Stack a Backbone

Robin A. Jones, Ph.D.

Order this book online at www.trafford.com
or email orders@trafford.com

Most Trafford titles are also available at major online book retailers.

Print information available on the last page.

ISBN: 978-1-4907-8879-1 (sc)

Trafford rev. 12/29/2018

www.trafford.com

North America & international
toll-free: 1 888 232 4444 (USA & Canada)
fax: 812 355 4082

Dedicated to #TwiceExceptionalStudents

This is YOUR life, live it.

Prologue

This is a dedication to children of whom are considered Twice Exceptional or 2E. Over the past few years, as a person who believes in a fair and equitable education for all, I have learned that there are many students who learn differently due to a high cognitive ability.

As each school year ends and many graduate from various levels within K-12, most specifically high school and college, I hope and pray there will be many memories and personalities in the one-liners within the context of this book to aid them in their lifetime. Anonymously, please allow me to share with you a couple of my students. The names are changed to protect the innocent.

I have been teaching in K-12, both in California, and Ohio. I recall one of my students which I recruited into my classroom while he was in kindergarten. He was referred to as Little Johnny. Each day as I arrived to teach in my classroom, Little Johnny was seated in the hallway. When I questioned the rationale for placing a kindergarten student in the hallway rather than the classroom, I was told, "Little Johnny would not complete his work, and he was disruptive." I petitioned to place Little Johnny in my classroom. From that point forward, Little Johnny was always the first student to complete his work, and complete it correctly. It was at that time, I realized many students were not given a fair chance at learning. So, I always asked myself, "Was Little Johnny disruptive, or bored?"

On another occasion, I met a student who's referred to as Steven. He was a middle school student with a customized education plan, known as an IEP. Steven was a chronic absentee. When Steven attended class, he was very anxious; always playing while receiving zero scores on his work. The counselor told me he was a slow learner. After spending just 15 minutes with Steven, I realized he was not a slow learner. Steven was having a significant amount of home problems. He did not have a dad. His mother was in prison. He was being raised by a grandmother who also had two of his cousins. Steven was a product of his environment. I made a pact with Steven, and asked him to promise me that if he would improve his attendance, I would help him pass on to the seventh grade. From that point forward, Steven had a 100% attendance. His assessment scores improved by 20%, and he passed on to the seventh grade.

My last case reference includes a young child referred to as Jimmy, who was a rambunctious young toddler. He was always active and full of 'busyness'.

When Jimmy started preschool, it was a never ending battle to keep him engaged with the class lessons and minimize his disruption. After four preschools in six months Jimmy's mother decided to remove him and allow Jimmy to receive a homeschool curriculum until he reached the age of kindergarten. When Jimmy started kindergarten, it was noticeable that his teacher had a difficult time with Jimmy. Jimmy was very anxious in the classroom which caused the remaining students to mimic his behavior. Eventually assessments were given as an opportunity for his mother to adapt to his recommended educational interventions. Jimmy eventually navigated his way through the various educational programs and became a model student. Jimmy went on to become class valedictorian, graduated high school and enrolled in college.

With each of the above case studies it was noted that the children of whom were thought to be less than stellar in the classroom, could potentially be considered 2E. Students who are considered 2E have medical and educational diagnoses of various behavior anxieties and/or disabilities, which may also include learning pattern disorders that do not match the conventional educational programs in the K-12 environment. Most 2E students will have a diagnosis with a high cognitive ability or gifted intelligence which leaves them vulnerable within the educational system. With the latter, the teacher may not understand which disability to include for the delivery of the curriculum.

In order to meet with a successful outcome for 2E students each family needs to be included into the educational intervention to ensure the child's success in life. It is important to understand and to work through all areas of the child's disabilities, or their Twice Exceptional status according to the United States Department of Education (USED, 2015). In the above cases, the students were more than a disruption with an isolated disability; they were extremely smart. So, begs the question (Jones, 2014): "When a student has a disability with a high cognitive ability, is the student gifted and bored, or both?"

As a teacher in the general classroom, I always explain to my students, "No one gives you a pass in life - there are no excuses." It was important for them to understand the importance to keep moving forward, in spite of the tags and labels that people will throw at you. You should always embrace who you are and whose you are.

All students regardless of your learning abilities, should remember that you and only you, have the ability to make your own life choices and no one else should make them or define them for you. Understand that a label is something others see, that is not what or who you are.

For Little Johnny, I remember leaving school for the end of the year, and I heard a voice shouting at me from across the parking lot: "Thank you Dr. J for all your work and helping Little Johnny." It was Little Johnny's sister who gave me the biggest hug from his grandmother.

For Steven, by the time he entered middle school his mother was no longer incarcerated. He enrolled into a summer school program, and he was noted as the 'Best Student' in his graduating class.

For Jimmy, when he finished the seventh grade, he was given the opportunity to skip eighth grade and transition immediately into high school. Fast forward, he continued on with high school and at the age of 16, while still enrolled in his sophomore year, Jimmy started his college career as a part-time student at the local community college. Jimmy plans on studying political science for his undergraduate program and hopefully enter law school.

#TwiceExceptionalStudents

References:

Jones, R. (2014). Relationship of Teacher Training Levels to Teacher Referrals for Twice Exceptional. Published manuscript, Proquest database. Psychology, Behavioral and Social Science. Walden University, Minnesota.

United States Department of Education (USED, 2015) U.S. Department of Education. A Nation Accountable: Twenty-five Years After A Nation at Risk, Washington, D.C.: Retrieved from http://www.ed.gov/rschstat/research/pubs/accountable/ http://www2.ed.gov/rschstat/research/pubs/accountable/accountable.pdf

1. Take advantage of the one big chance. **#ItIsYourOpportunity**

2. When they show you who they are – believe them. **#TakeOffRunning**

3. Saturate others with love. **#LiveAsThoughThisIsYourLastDay**

4. Never follow a path - make your own trail. **#LeadYourOwnJourney**

5. What you want in life may not be what you get. **#ThereIsAlwaysAnotherDay**

Notes

_____

_____

_____

_____

Notes

6. 'Please' and 'thank you' are two of your most important words. **#SayThemOften**

7. Conversations are a work of art. **#TakeTimeToListen**

8. Don't allow a wishbone grow where a backbone should be. **#BeHonestButFirm**

9. If you break it you buy it. **#YouCannotAffordToBorrowIt**

10. Never criticize or condemn another person. **#TryToWalkInTheirShoes**

Notes

_____

_____

_____

_____

_____

11. Never be afraid to ask out the best looking girl in the room. **#BeautyAndBrains**

12. Learn to appreciate the small things. **#ItIsTheThoughtThatCounts**

13. Best things in life are free. **#UnderstandTheValueOfASunrise**

14. When a loved one transitions ask how you may help. **#WhatCanIDo**

15. Every book has chapters. **#WhichOneDidYouWriteForYourLife**

Notes

_____

_____

_____

_____

_____

16. You were born a miracle. **#MakeTheMostOfIt**

17. Respect your parents. **#TheyWillAlwaysBeThereForYou**

18. Hard times will come and go. **#MoneyDoesNotLastAlways**

19. Everyone will experience death. **#SuddenOrTerminal**

20. Look in the mirror. **#WhatDoYouSee**

Notes

_____

_____

_____

_____

_____

21. Always stand to shake hands. **#SittingIsNotAnOption**

22. Don't fill up on bread. **#EatInPortions**

23. In a negotiation, never make the first offer. **#AlwaysCounter**

24. Know what you want to do. **#ActLikeYouHaveBeenThereBefore**

25. Request the late check-out. **#YouWillNotRegretIt**

Notes

_____

_____

_____

_____

Notes

26. When entrusted with a secret, keep it. **#ShowConfidentiality**

27. Ask for a mentor. **#HoldYourHeroesToAHigherStandard**

28. Return a borrowed car with a full tank of gas. **#RespectIsAVirtue**

29. Shake hands and look the person in the eyes. **#EyesAreTheWindowToTheSoul**

30. It takes seven "NO's" to get to "YES". **#KeepAsking**

Notes

_____

_____

_____

_____

31.   If you need music on the beach, you're missing the point. **#DoYouGetIt**

32.   Handkerchiefs are classy. **#MakeSureTheyAreClean**

33.   Marry the girl you love. **#YouWillMarryHerWholeFamily**

34.   When expressing condolences, ask no questions. **#SoSorryForYourLoss**

35.   Remain calm on the surface and paddle like crazy underneath. **#BeLikeADuck**

Notes

_____

_____

_____

_____

_____

36. Experience the serenity of traveling alone. **#KnowYourself**

37. Never turn down a breath mint. **#TakeIt**

38. A sport coat is worth 1000 words. **#ATailoredSuitIsWorthTheInvestment**

39. Try writing your own eulogy. **#NeverStopRevising**

40. Thank a veteran. **#AndThenMakeItUpToThem**

Notes

_____

_____

_____

_____

41.   Know what makes you unique. **#SitForACaricatureDrawing**

42.   Eat lunch with the new kid. **#YouWillLearnSomething**

43.   After writing an angry email, read it carefully. **#ThenDeleteIt**

44.   Give credit. **#TakeTheBlame**

45.   Write down your dreams. **#YouWillLiveThemOneDay**

Notes

_____

_____

_____

_____

_____

Notes

_____

_____

_____

_____

_____

_____

_____

_____

_____

_____

_____

_____

_____

_____

_____

_____

46.   Never tell yourself no; just not right now. **#LearnFromYourLessons**

47.   Work like it's all up to you, and pray like it's all up to God. **#ChangeIsEmminent**

48.   Your belt should match your shoes. **#WearOne**

49.   Listen twice as much as you speak. **#YouCannotHearWhenYouAreTalking**

50.   People are more important than things. **#YouCryOverALife**

Notes

_____

_____

_____

_____

_____

51.   If you need a lifeline. **#CallSomeoneYouLove**

52.   When you drive, learn to take your time. **#TicketsAreCostly**

53.   An apology is not a sign of weakness. **#ItShowsIntegrity**

54.   Respect your parents and those who have rule over you. **#FeedbackIsPriceless**

55.   Never throw the first punch. **#Don'tWalk AwayAndLeaveYourOpponentStanding**

Notes

_____

_____

_____

_____

56.   Women are not your punching bag. **#RememberYou MayHaveADaughterSomeday**

57.   Be kind to all you meet. **#YouMayBeInPositionToHelpOrReceive**

58.   If it goes up. **#ItWillComeDown**

59.   You should always learn something from someone. **#GoodBadIndifferent**

60.   Read the book, "Who's holding your Ladder?" **#BySamChand**

Notes

_____

_____

_____

_____

_____

61. Never criticize or condemn another person. **#LifeCanBePainful**

62. Education does not have a stopping point. **#BecomeAStudentAlways**

63. No one is exempt when getting out of bed. **#AlwaysFeetFirst**

64. Love hard, talk soft, words cannot be replaced. **#TheTongueIsLikeASword**

65. Know that a child somewhere is watching. **#ChildrenAreTheFuture**

Notes

_____

_____

_____

_____

_____

Notes

_____

_____

_____

_____

_____

_____

_____

_____

_____

_____

_____

_____

_____

_____

66.   Never burn a bridge. **#YouMayNeedToCrossItAgain**

67.   Be bold, be brave. **#StandStrong**

68.   Waking up in a warm bed is a privilege. **#ItIsNotARight**

69.   What am I doing to affect change? **#AskYourselfDaily**

70.   Sometime you just have to go with the flow. **#EnjoyTheRide**

Notes

_____

_____

_____

_____

71. Kind words cost nothing. **#InappropriateCommentsLeaveScars**

72. For every action there is a reaction. **#LetTheMirrorReflect**

73. The race was not given to the swift. **#RememberTheTortoiseAndTheHare**

74. Keep in mind, it starts with one. **#MakeADifference**

75. Our skin color may be different. **#WeAllBleedRed**

Notes

_____

_____

_____

_____

76. Be like a sponge and absorb as much as possible. **#LifeIsAJourneyOfLessons**

77. Hold your head high. **#StayPositive**

78. Don't wish for the life of another person. **#EveryoneIsFightingSomeKindofBattle**

79. Pick yourself up! **#GetBackOnTheHorse**

80. Body hygiene is important. **#WearCleanClothes**

Notes

_____

_____

_____

_____

_____

81.　Never allow disrespect. **#StandUpSpeakUp**

82.　Brush your teeth and get your annual eye exam. **#YouOnlyGetOneSet**

83.　Your attitude sets your altitude. **#RemainPositiveAndHopeful**

84.　Grace and mercy go hand in hand with faith and hope. **#ThereIsAHigherPower**

85.　Get to know Christ at an early age. **#PrayDaily**

Notes

_____

_____

_____

_____

_____

Notes

_____

_____

_____

_____

_____

_____

_____

_____

_____

_____

_____

_____

_____

_____

_____

_____

_____

86. Be a thought leader in your own space. **#YouAreAnExpert**

87. No need to be the best in everything. **#JustBeTheBestInWhatYouDo**

88. Sometimes accomplishments are made in baby steps. **#OneDayAtATime**

89. Give back - YES - Give back. **#PayItForward**

90. Choose your words wisely. **#SomeWordsNeedNotBeSaid**

Notes

_____

_____

_____

_____

91. Set your current goal; plan your next goal. **#KnowWhereYouWantToGo**

92. Celebrate even the smallest of victories. **#TheyAreAllImportant**

93. Say "YES" rather than "YEA". **#ItWillShowRespect**

94. Say "THANK YOU" rather than "THANKS". **#WhyNot**

95. Arrive on time. **#AllowForDelays**

Notes

---

96.   Remember, it is not what you say. **#ItIsHowYouSayIt**

97.   Remember the elderly. **#TheyPavedTheWay**

98.   Sit up straight. **#LiveLaughLove**

99.   Get a partner who is willing to make a sacrifice. **#LoveIsImportant**

100.   Put your electronic device DOWN when at the dinner table. **#ShowOthersYouCare**

Notes

_____

_____

_____

_____

_____

101.   When driving, be kind, thoughtful and courteous. **#WatchOutForTheNextDriver**

102.   Be courteous to others. **#ItIsAWorkofArt**

103.   Foul language is ugly. **#StayCalm**

104.   Restroom courtesy – wash your hands. **#MessyIsNotCool**

105.   When entering a room, always speak to others. **#IntroduceYourself**

Notes

_____

_____

_____

_____

Notes

_____

_____

_____

_____

_____

_____

_____

_____

_____

_____

_____

_____

_____

106.   Love your body regardless of your perceived fallacies. **#YouOnlyHaveOne**

107.   A dog that brings a bone will carry one. **#BridleYourTongueOfOthers**

108.   If you gossip with me, you will gossip about me. **#IsItKindNecessaryOrNice**

109.   Racism is rooted into ignorance. **#EducateYourself**

110.   Everyone is dealing with something. **#LifeIsA@@@@@**

Notes

_____

_____

_____

_____

111. Follow your passion. **#YourHeartWillLeadYou**

112. Privacy is a must. **#RespectTheSpaceOfOthers**

113. Understand that taking risks can reap benefits or failures. **#ChooseWisely**

114. Be genuine - trust others. **#StandUpForYourBeliefs**

115. Honesty and respect are always your "go-to". **#WhichOneAreYou**

Notes

_____

_____

_____

_____

116.   Patience and practice goes a long way. **#ThinkAboutIt**

117.   It is better to ask forgiveness than permission. **#OrIsIt**

118.   There is always a loser. **#TroubleDoesNotLastAlways**

119.   Be polite and always show respect to others. **#QuidProQuo**

120.   Remember to use your table manners. **#NoSmackingNoSlurping**

Notes

_____

_____

_____

_____

_____

121.   Know how to use your napkin. **#TheNapkinTellsWhenYouAreFinished**

122.   Never reach across the dinner table. **#AskForTheDishYouWant**

123.   Trusting your gut can be good and bad. **#InstinctsAreReal**

124.   When in the presence of others make introductions. **#KnowTheirNames**

125.   Be strong enough that people know your will. **#StandYourGround**

Notes

_____

_____

_____

_____

_____

Notes

126. Saying 'excuse me' covers a multiple of faults. **#SayItOften**

127. Kindness is given. **#RudenessIsNotAcceptable**

128. Being polite is free. **#ThereIsNoCost**

129. Learn from your mistakes. **#SecondTimeCouldBeConstruedAsIntentional**

130. Know that the light at the end of the tunnel is not a train. **#ItIsYourGuidingStar**

Notes

_____

_____

_____

_____

131. Keep your friends close and your enemies closer. **#KnowWhomToTrust**

132. Walk beside your partner. **#TogethernessGoesFar**

133. The loss of a loved one will change your life forever. **#AppreciateEveryMoment**

134. Learn to say, "I'm sorry". **#AlwaysRememberWhoIsThereForYou**

135. Cooking is not gender specific. **#KnowHowToBoilWater**

Notes

_____

_____

_____

_____

_____

136.   Condoms will save your life. **#UseThem**

137.   Sexting is a federal crime. **#SoIsUninvitedSex**

138.   When driving respect the laws of the road. **#ObeyTheLawsOfTheLand**

139.   Remember that everyone you meet is not your friend. **#GoWithYourGut**

140.   Jealousy and envy is not a positive trait. **#BeGladForTheSuccessOfOthers**

Notes

_____

_____

_____

_____

_____

141. Connect with nature and get your vibes. **#LiveHappyLikeTheBirds**

142. Having a loving family cannot be purchased or replaced. **#LoveWithoutCondition**

143. Just grin and bear it! **#LifeIsGood**

144. Do not allow the opinions of others to consume you. **#OpinionsAreWithoutFacts**

145. Keep moving forward. **#YourPastHasPassed**

Notes

_____

_____

_____

_____

Notes

_____

_____

_____

_____

_____

_____

_____

_____

_____

_____

_____

_____

_____

_____

_____

146.   Accepting drinks from others is a "NO-NO". **#DoNotLeaveYourDrinkUnattended**

147.   Using drugs, illegal or prescription, is a choice. **#YouAreFightingALosingBattle**

148.   It is never too late to start. **#JustDoIt**

149.   Life is like a ball game. **#HitTheCurveBalls**

150.   Ask what you do not know. **#IfYouDoNotAskYouWillNotKnow**

Notes

_____

_____

_____

_____

151.   Know the "FRIEND CODE". **#SomeSituationsCanBePrevented**

152.   Build a possy of friends. **#MoveAsAUnit**

153.   Remain alert and aware of your surroundings at all times. **#StayFocused**

154.   If you do not have the cash to make the purchase – WAIT. **#WaitForIt**

155.   Credit is a good thing; it can also be a not so good thing. **#PayBillsOnTime**

Notes

_____

_____

_____

_____

156. Marry your best friend. **#YouWillNotGoWrong**

157. Stay calm when stopped by any local enforcement officer. **#KnowYourRights**

158. It is always too early to give up. **#NeverTooLateToStart**

159. Celebrate victoriously. **#ItWillComeSoon**

160. Courage is yours. **#TakeIt**

Notes

_____

_____

_____

_____

_____

161. Believe in yourself. **#YourBestIsYetToCome**

162. Accept failures. **#TheyMakeYouStronger**

163. Stay together when out and about. **#DoNotLeaveWithARandomPerson**

164. If your friend is drinking – both cannot drink. **#MoreThanTwoDrinksAreTooMany**

165. Easy removes the challenge. **#ItDoesNotDefineYou**

Notes

_____

_____

_____

_____

_____

Notes

166. Register to vote. **#MakeYourVoiceHeard**

167. Never meet a stranger. **#MakeFriends**

168. Love yourself. **#DoNotAllowForIntrusion**

169. Confidence without attitude. **#KnowWhoAndWhomYouAre**

170. Ask your questions. **#IfUnsureAskAgain**

Notes

---

171.   Pay it forward. **#RememberFromWhenceYouCame**

172.   Buy your own home. **#EnjoyTheLuxuriesofLife**

173.   Know what you want and go get it. **#SetTheBarHigh**

174.   Learn the lessons of life. **#SewingCookingDrivingWoodworking**

175.   If you arrive together – leave together. **#DoNotGoHomeAlone**

Notes

_____

_____

_____

_____

176.   Know how to read a map. **#GPSSystemsSometimesFail**

177.   Live without regret. **#YouMayRegretTheChancesYouDidNotTake**

178.   Go past the crowd. **#SetYourOwnPace**

179.   There is no substitution for sleep. **#GetYourRest**

180.   Exercise your brain. **#EngageInWordGames**

Notes

_____

_____

_____

_____

_____

181. A broken light bulb shatters into a thousand pieces. **#SoDoesABrokenHeart**

182. Eat what you want. **#YouAreWhatYouEat**

183. Start your bucket list. **#ItIsNeverTooEarly**

184. Rules are made to be broken. **#SetExpectationsRatherThanRules**

185. Be confident with your message. **#LearnToExcel**

Notes

_____

_____

_____

_____

Notes

_____

_____

_____

_____

_____

_____

_____

_____

_____

_____

_____

_____

_____

_____

186.   Do not ask 'WHY', ask 'Why NOT'. **#IncreaseYourWorthOfKnowledge**

187.   The latest trends come and go. **#DressForSuccess**

188.   Give unconditionally without expectations. **#DoNotLoseYourMorals**

189.   Dishonesty is not a trait to borrow. **#BeTrueToYourself**

190.   Maintain your values. **#DoNotCompromise**

Notes

_____

_____

_____

_____

_____

191. Follow the rainbow. **#GetYourPotOfGold**

192. Know the gentleman's agreement. **#YourWordIsYourBond**

193. Play with those whose skills are stronger than yours. **#YouWillOnlyGetBetter**

194. Do not take kindness for a weakness. **#BeFlexible**

195. People have time for what they want to do. **#WhatGoesAroundComesAround**

Notes

_____

_____

_____

_____

196. You will get there. **#DontSweatTheSmallStuff**

197. You may not be one of them. **#AskForHelp**

198. Think positive – stay focused. **#YourTimeWillCome**

199. Don't settle or don't lose your morals. **#ConfrontThoseWhoChallengeYou**

200. Avoid demands. **#LetGoLetGod**

Notes

_____

_____

_____

_____

_____

201.   Make lists. **#GetOrganized**

202.   Do not be fearful. **#TheOnlyConstantIsChange**

203.   What is your hobby? **#GetOne**

204.   No, means no, means no. **#LearnToSayNO**

205.   Problems are challenges. **#BeFlexible**

Notes

_____

_____

_____

_____

_____

Notes

206.   Get up earlier. **#SuccessStartsWhenOthersAreSleeping**

207.   Do not get distracted. **#CryIfNecessary**

208.   Reflect on your joys. **#TimeHealsAllWounds**

209.   Choose wisely, you are judged accordingly. **#DoNotAllowOthersToCondemnYou**

210.   There will be struggles before the breakthrough. **#SmileThroughThem**

Notes

_____

_____

_____

_____

_____

211. Learn to face your fears. **#TakeOnChallenges**

212. You cannot spell challenge without change. **#DoSomething**

213. Pretend you are living your last day. **#AskYourselfWhatChangesWouldIMake**

214. Siblings are your best friends. **#NeverAllowOthersToCreateDistanceBetweenYou**

215. Be aware of your surroundings. **#YouNeverKnowWhetherSomeoneIsWatching**

Notes

_____

_____

_____

_____

_____

Notes

Stand for your beliefs or you will fall for anything.

#StackABackbone

Be courageous - #StepOutOnLife

About the author:

Robin A. Jones noted many students throughout her teaching career, who were not provided with an effective learning opportunity due to reading challenges or behavior disorders only to later discover they were not in a learner-centered environment. The case studies noted in the prologue were the inspiration for her to return to college and receive her Doctorate of Philosophy majoring in Psychology and Education to study children with disabilities who are gifted and disabled. with anxieties, also referred to as Twice Exceptional. Dr. Jones believes that every student has the potential to not only learn but to be successful in life.

She has a commitment to strong work ethics, education, and a passion for entrepreneurship. Her career path started with General Electric as a database developer building her first database for the F14 Aircraft Fighter planes and from there her career eventually catapulted her way to the position of Interim CIO.

In her 40+ years of employment in technology, Robin spent 12 of those years gainfully employed as founder and entrepreneur of a multimillion dollar company which received national awards and presidential recognition.

From there, Robin's career advanced to fortune 50 companies such as IBM, Ashland Oil, and the U.S. Departments of Energy, and Defense. In her most recent capacity, Robin retired from University of California, Berkeley - Haas School of Business, Computer Center as Senior Manager, PMO Director.

Today, Robin continues to work in the field of higher education as an Associate Professor, and she is a strong advocate for children in K-12 who are Twice Exceptional. She has a hobby of collecting exotic sunrises and sunsets as depicted throughout the book.

She is the proud auntie of nine nieces and nephews and six greats and refers to them as her strength and endurance trainers. Throughout life we all receive curveballs which we are required to overcome. Robin's curveball and greatest accomplishment is surviving breast cancer; not once, but twice. All thanks to God and His Glory.

Notes

Printed in the United States
By Bookmasters